Especially For:

_____

_____

_____

MIGHTY BIG AND SUPER GREAT:
TEXAS
IS THE
"LONE STAR STATE"!

Written by
Amber Manning

Illustrated by
Kory Fluckiger

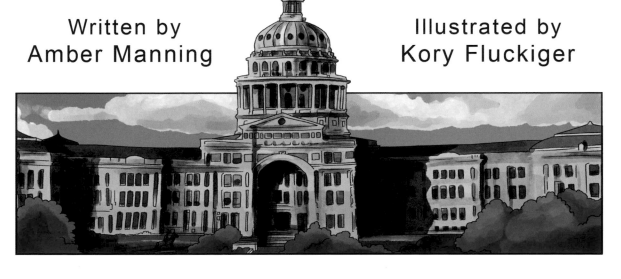

Published by Bluebonnet Kids™
A Registered Trademark Imprint
1836 Spirit of Texas Way Suite 200 Conroe, TX 77301

Published by Bluebonnet Kids™
A Registered Trademark Imprint
1836 Spirit of Texas Way, Suite 200 Conroe, TX 77301

Library of Congress Cataloging-in-Publication Data is available.

For information about bulk purchases, please email: admin@bluebonnetkids.com
For more information about the Author visit: www.bluebonnetkids.com

LCCN: 2017908673
ISBN 97809987704-4-4 (HB)
ISBN 978-0-9987704-0-6 (eBook)

Printed in Canada

To schedule a school visit, please contact Amber Manning (ambermanningtxauthor@yahoo.com).

Dedicated to all the little cowboys and cowgirls of our great state.
To my boys, you are my whole world. Without you, I wouldn't be me.
You have all my love...always. May you grow up to be respectful,
good-hearted, successful "Texas" gentlemen.
To my boss, David Thomas Roberts, thank you for giving me the
opportunity to make my dreams come true.
To my family and friends who stood behind me though my failures and
successes, thank you for your support. I love you.
My son once asked when he was about four, "Mommy, does everybody
in the world live in Texas?" I replied, "No, but they should."

Acknowledgements:
Janet Musick, David Thomas Roberts and Tanya Roberts

Fight, fight, win!!
In 1836, we begin...
At the Battle of San Jacinto,
In remembrance of the Alamo.

Texas became a Republic that year;
Our victory was cause for cheer!
For we had won the long, hard fight...
To claim our independence right!!

Many thanks to Sam Houston, Juan Seguín...
And every hero in between.
Bowie, Travis and Crockett fought hard to defend;
They were strong and courageous men.

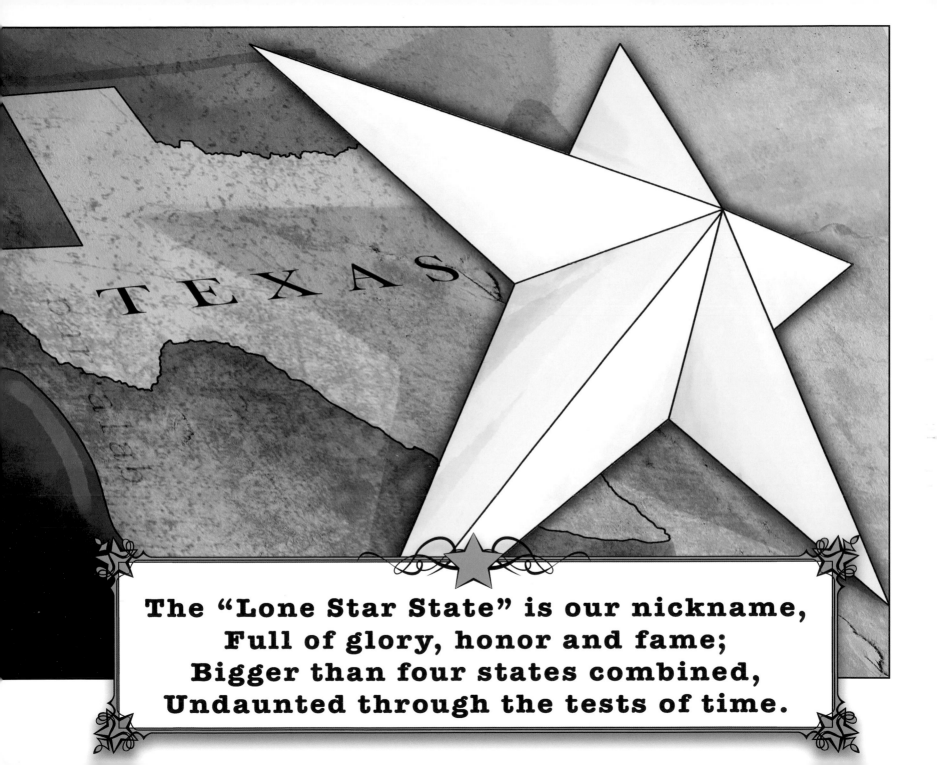

The "Lone Star State" is our nickname,
Full of glory, honor and fame;
Bigger than four states combined,
Undaunted through the tests of time.

**Stephen F. Austin was the man...
Who brought law and settlers to our land.
Austin is our capital city;
Our capitol building stands tall and pretty!!**

The Texas flag, red, white, and blue...
Represents the Texas true.
Our flag waves in symbolic glory;
For our heroes, it remembers their story.

On our flag, a single star,
Is what truly sets us apart.
Beside the Stars and Stripes it is flown,
Showing we can stand alone.

For bravery, our stripe is red.
The blue, for loyalty we spread.
Our flag's third color is bright and white;
It stands for the purity to do what's right.

Ever heard of the Texas Rangers?
They help us out when we're in danger;
Sharpest men you've ever seen...
With skills superb and eyes so keen!

Our motto is friendship and it begins...
From the word "Tejas," which means friends.
The bluebonnet, which is our state flower,
Can simply be enjoyed for hours.

The Texas mammal, the armadillo,
Is found from Brownsville to Amarillo.
Houston sent men to the moon...
And we make great country tunes.

The boys in cowboy hats are nice,
But cowgirls, they are "sugar and spice"!
Rodeo is our favorite state sport;
Those big bulls can buck and snort!

In Texas, we produce cows, cotton and sheep;
We lead that production by a huge leap!
Because we make these things it is known,
Texas can always take care of its own!!

Texas produces lots of oil;
It comes from down underneath the soil!
It started shooting up out of the ground!!
At the Spindletop well, it was found.

Texas has many sights to see,
Mountains like Guadalupe Peak!
There are rivers and lakes too,
Refreshing to take the scenic view.

Caddo Lake's our natural lake;
The many beautiful pictures we could take.
We also have the Great Plains,
Canyons too, and fields of grain.

From butterflies to mockingbirds...
And the ranches with our longhorn herds,
Texas stretches far and wide...
And it fills our hearts with pride.

Folks around here are proud to say...
We do things the "Texas" way!
Where friendships last and cattle roam,
Texas is our "Home Sweet Home".

Fun Texas Facts

⭐ The Texas flower is the Bluebonnet.

⭐ The Monarch butterfly is the official insect of Texas. (What changes into a butterfly? Do you know?)

⭐ The official bird of Texas is the mockingbird.

⭐ The official large mammal is the longhorn.

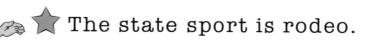

⭐ The state sport is rodeo.

⭐ The dish of Texas is chili.

⭐ The State Fair Park in Dallas, Texas has the LARGEST ferris wheel in the Western Hemisphere. (Have you ever ridden on a ferris wheel?)

⭐ Texas has more airports than any other state.

⭐ The longest river in Texas is the Rio Grande, at 1270 miles long.

★ The most popular snacks in Texas are: Frito pie, peanuts in Dr Pepper, beef jerky, jalapenos and corn dogs. (Peanuts in Dr Pepper?? That's funny!)

★ About 70% of the population of Texas lives within 200 miles of Austin. (I do. Do you?)

★ Austin is considered to be the "live music capital of the world".

★ Caddo Lake is the only natural lake in Texas. All others are manmade.

★ Guadalupe Peak is approximately 8751 feet tall and the highest point in Texas. (Whoa! That's really tall.)

★ The King Ranch of Texas is larger than the entire state of Rhode Island!

★ Sam Rayburn Reservoir is the largest body of water completely in Texas.

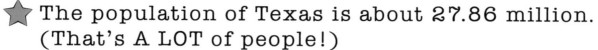

★ The population of Texas is about 27.86 million. (That's A LOT of people!)

★ There are nearly 12.3 million cows in Texas. (Almost as many cows as people!)

★ The Tyler Municipal Rose Garden is the world's largest rose garden. There are 500 varieties on 14 acres. A total of 35,000 rose bushes.

★ The second largest rock in the nation is Enchanted Rock which has an exposed surface area of 130 square miles, which lies on the border between Gillespie and Llano Counties, Texas.

★ Texas is as large as all of New England, New York, Pennsylvania, Ohio and Illinois combined. That is bigger than 5 states combined!!

★ The all American meal, the hamburger, was created in Athens, Texas.

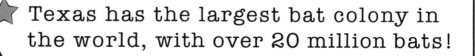

★ Texas has the largest bat colony in the world, with over 20 million bats!

★ The Amarillo airport has the 3rd largest runway in the world and is designated as an alternate landing site for the space shuttle.

★ Texas has 90 mountains a mile or more high, with Guadalupe Peak in West Texas being the tallest.

★ Texas has four national forests – Angelina, Davy Crockett, Sabine and Sam Houston and two national parks – Big Bend and Guadalupe Mountains.

★ The tidewater of Texas stretches 624 miles along the Gulf of Mexico and is the site of 600 or more historic shipwrecks.

★ The Seven Wonders of Texas are: The Natural Bridge Caverns, Enchanted Rock, Big Bend National Park, Padre Island National Seashore, The Meteor Crater, Big Thicket National Preserve, and the Palo Duro Canyon State Park.

10 QUESTIONS
ABOUT TEXAS AND THIS BOOK

⭐ How many times did you see the Texas flag in this book?

⭐ How many times did you see the state of Texas?

⭐ What is the capital of Texas?

⭐ Who wrote this book (Author)?

⭐ Who created the pictures in this book (Illustrator)?

⭐ What was your favorite thing to learn about Texas?

⭐ Who was the Father of Texas?

⭐ What's the oldest law enforcement agency in Texas?

⭐ What is the state motto of Texas?

⭐ What is Texas' nickname?

Texas Pledge
(say it with me)

"Honor the Texas flag; I pledge allegiance to thee, Texas, one and indivisible."

Texas Song
Texas, Our Texas

"Texas, our Texas!
All hail the mighty state!
Texas, our Texas!
So wonderful, so great!

Boldest and grandest,
withstanding every test;
O empire wide and glorious,
you stand supremely blest.

(CHORUS)
God bless you, Texas!
And keep you brave and strong.
That you may grow in power and worth,
throughout the ages long. Texas,

O Texas!
Your freeborn single star.
Sends out its radiance
to nations near and far.

Emblem of freedom!
It sets our hearts aglow.
With thoughts of San Jacinto
and the glorious Alamo.

Texas, dear Texas!
From tyrant grip now free,
Shines forth in splendor
your star of destiny!

Mother of heroes!
We come your children true.
Proclaiming our allegiance,
our faith, our love for you."

written by
Marsh and Gladys Yoakum Wright